NEVER ENOUGH
Separating Self-Worth from Approval

COMPANION WORKBOOK
ideas for reflection

LEARN HOW TO BLOOM
from your inner wisdom and strength
— & —
feel the universe supporting you as you do!

Deb Lang, Psy.D.

Copyright © 2022 by Deb Lang, Psy.D.

All rights reserved. This book or any portion thereof may not be reproduced or used in any manner whatsoever without the express written permission of the publisher except for the use of brief quotations in a book review.

Printed in the United States of America First Printing, 2022

ISBN: 978-1-7371274-3-7

Disclaimer: The information shared in this book is for educational and informational purposes only and is not intended to be viewed as medical or mental health advice. It is not designed to be a substitute for professional advice from your physician, therapist, attorney, accountant or any other health care practitioner or licensed professional. Providing you with this information does not mean that you have a therapist/client relationship with the Author.

The Publisher and the Author do not make any guarantees as to the effectiveness of any of the techniques, suggestions, tips, ideas or strategies shared in this book as each situation differs.

The Publisher and Author shall neither have liability nor responsibility with respect to any direct or indirect loss or damage caused or alleged by the information shared in this book related to your health, life or business or any other aspect of your situation. It's your responsibility to do your own due diligence and use your own judgment when applying any techniques or situations mentioned in or through this book.

introduction

Use this journal in any way that feels responsive to you. I have offered questions, for each chapter, designed to help you think about and apply what you are reading to your own life.

You might write out your answers, or, if you are more visual, you might draw something that depicts your reaction to a question.

Before moving on to the questions, take a few moments to reflect on your hopes for yourself in reading this book. In what ways do you hope to bloom? Write those ideas down in the space below.

I'm sending my caring and support as you plant the seeds to blossom and bloom in a way that only you can bloom!

Ideas for Reflection: A Companion Workbook to *Never Enough - Separating Self-Worth from Approval* by Deb Lang, Psy.D.

Ideas for Reflection: A Companion Workbook to *Never Enough - Separating Self-Worth from Approval*
by Deb Lang, Psy.D.

chapter one
notes

Ideas for Reflection: A Companion Workbook to *Never Enough - Separating Self-Worth from Approval* by Deb Lang, PsyD.

chapter one
notes

Ideas for Reflection: A Companion Workbook to *Never Enough - Separating Self-Worth from Approval*
by Deb Lang, PsyD.

chapter one
reflections

In what ways do you work hard to be "enough?"

_____

_____

_____

_____

_____

_____

_____

_____

_____

_____

_____

_____

_____

_____

_____

_____

Ideas for Reflection: A Companion Workbook to *Never Enough - Separating Self-Worth from Approval*
by Deb Lang, Psy.D.

chapter one
reflections

What impact has the striving you have been doing to be good enough had on you, both emotionally and physically?

Ideas for Reflection: A Companion Workbook to *Never Enough - Separating Self-Worth from Approval* by Deb Lang, Psy.D.

chapter one
reflections

In what ways have you blamed yourself for looking outside of yourself for approval?

_____

_____

_____

_____

_____

_____

_____

_____

_____

_____

_____

_____

_____

_____

_____

Ideas for Reflection: A Companion Workbook to *Never Enough - Separating Self-Worth from Approval* by Deb Lang, Psy.D.

chapter two
part one
notes

Ideas for Reflection: A Companion Workbook to *Never Enough - Separating Self-Worth from Approval* by Deb Lang, Psy.D.

chapter two
part one
notes

chapter two
part one
reflections

What feelings came up as you read this section?

_____
_____
_____
_____
_____
_____
_____
_____
_____
_____
_____
_____
_____
_____
_____
_____
_____
_____

Ideas for Reflection: A Companion Workbook to *Never Enough - Separating Self-Worth from Approval*
by Deb Lang, Psy.D.

chapter two
part one
reflections

In what ways were you socialized to please, look pretty, or to keep the peace?

Ideas for Reflection: A Companion Workbook to *Never Enough - Separating Self-Worth from Approval* by Deb Lang, Psy.D.

chapter two
part one
reflections

In what ways have you been afraid to be yourself or felt fearful of speaking up because of being female?

Ideas for Reflection: A Companion Workbook to *Never Enough - Separating Self-Worth from Approval* by Deb Lang, Psy.D.

chapter two
part two
notes

chapter two
part two
notes

Ideas for Reflection: A Companion Workbook to *Never Enough - Separating Self-Worth from Approval*
by Deb Lang, PsyD.

chapter two
part two
reflections

When and how did you learn what it means to be attractive?

Ideas for Reflection: A Companion Workbook to *Never Enough - Separating Self-Worth from Approval* by Deb Lang, Psy.D.

chapter two
part two
reflections

What pressures have you felt around your appearance or your weight?

Ideas for Reflection: A Companion Workbook to *Never Enough - Separating Self-Worth from Approval* by Deb Lang, PsyD.

chapter two
part two
reflections

In what ways do you seek approval through your appearance?

Ideas for Reflection: A Companion Workbook to *Never Enough - Separating Self-Worth from Approval* by Deb Lang, Psy.D.

chapter two
part two
reflections

What associations do you have with the word "fat?"

chapter two
part two
reflections

What reactions did you have to the ideas presented about weight and social hierarchies?

Ideas for Reflection: A Companion Workbook to *Never Enough - Separating Self-Worth from Approval* by Deb Lang, PsyD.

chapter two
part two
reflections

If you have tried unsuccessfully to lose weight, what assumptions have you made about yourself?

chapter two
part two
reflections

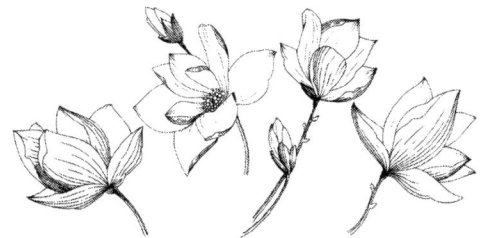

Take some time to think about your relationships. What qualities do you look for in a friend? Do any of these qualities have to do with appearance?

Ideas for Reflection: A Companion Workbook to *Never Enough - Separating Self-Worth from Approval* by Deb Lang, Psy.D.

chapter two
part two
reflections

How do the standards you hold for yourself for weight or appearance differ from those you hold for your daughter or a good friend? What was it like to realize that these standards simply reflect different pathways in the brain?

chapter two
part two
reflections

How might you use the information presented in this chapter to reconsider some of your assumptions about weight and appearance? What is an action you might take?

chapter two
part two
reflections

How might you light a candle of body acceptance in your own life?

chapter two
part three
notes

chapter two
part three
notes

chapter two
part three
reflections

How was it to learn that these pulls to look outside yourself for your value simply reflect well-traveled circuits in the brain and that the structure of your brain is changeable?

chapter two
part three
reflections

What came up for you when I said you can't make other people happy or control their feelings?

chapter two
part three
reflections

In what ways do you find yourself comparing yourself with other women?

Ideas for Reflection: A Companion Workbook to *Never Enough - Separating Self-Worth from Approval*
by Deb Lang, Psy.D.

chapter two
part three
reflections

Take a moment to imagine a life in which you could be yourself and feel supported by the women in your life. What would it feel like and look like? How would you be acting, behaving, and relating? If that is hard to imagine, no worries. We will work on it in part two of the book.

_____
_____
_____
_____
_____
_____
_____
_____
_____
_____
_____
_____
_____
_____

Ideas for Reflection: A Companion Workbook to *Never Enough - Separating Self-Worth from Approval* by Deb Lang, Psy.D.

chapter three
notes

Ideas for Reflection: A Companion Workbook to *Never Enough - Separating Self-Worth from Approval* by Deb Lang, Psy.D.

chapter three
notes

Ideas for Reflection: A Companion Workbook to *Never Enough - Separating Self-Worth from Approval*
by Deb Lang, Psy.D.

chapter three
reflections

What messages did you receive about being yourself when you were young?

chapter three
reflections

Did you have a sense there was a way you "should be?" In what ways did you get these messages?

Ideas for Reflection: A Companion Workbook to *Never Enough - Separating Self-Worth from Approval* by Deb Lang, Psy.D.

chapter three
reflections

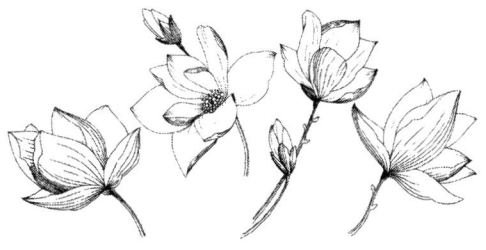

What impact have those messages had on you and your life?

Ideas for Reflection: A Companion Workbook to *Never Enough - Separating Self-Worth from Approval*
by Deb Lang, Psy.D.

chapter four
notes

chapter four
notes

Ideas for Reflection: A Companion Workbook to *Never Enough - Separating Self-Worth from Approval* by Deb Lang, Psy.D.

chapter four
reflections

In thinking about your early relationships, what did you learn about love and connection?

Ideas for Reflection: A Companion Workbook to *Never Enough - Separating Self-Worth from Approval* by Deb Lang, Psy.D.

chapter four
reflections

What does it mean to love someone, and how does that person know that you love them?

Ideas for Reflection: A Companion Workbook to *Never Enough - Separating Self-Worth from Approval* by Deb Lang, Psy.D.

chapter four
reflections

How might the pull to appease be impacting your life?

Ideas for Reflection: A Companion Workbook to *Never Enough - Separating Self-Worth from Approval* by Deb Lang, PsyD.

chapter four
reflections

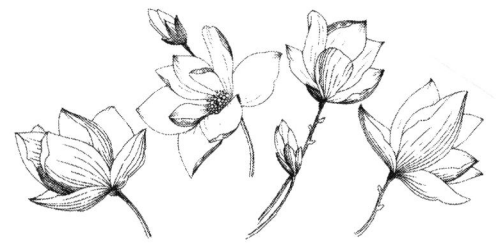

If you don't relate to the tendency to appease, does the thought of it bring up any fear?

Ideas for Reflection: A Companion Workbook to *Never Enough - Separating Self-Worth from Approval* by Deb Lang, Psy.D.

chapter five
notes

Ideas for Reflection: A Companion Workbook to Never Enough - Separating Self-Worth from Approval
by Deb Lang, Psy.D.

chapter five
notes

Ideas for Reflection: A Companion Workbook to *Never Enough - Separating Self-Worth from Approval*
by Deb Lang, Psy.D.

chapter five
reflections

Take a moment to think about the people you know. Have you known anyone who seems to have learned a disconnecting way of relating in relationships? If so, what feelings came up for you when interacting with them?

Ideas for Reflection: A Companion Workbook to *Never Enough - Separating Self-Worth from Approval* by Deb Lang, Psy.D.

chapter five
reflections

In what ways do you disconnect in relationships? Do you strike like a snake or slither away?

Ideas for Reflection: A Companion Workbook to *Never Enough - Separating Self-Worth from Approval*
by Deb Lang, PsyD.

chapter five
reflections

What do you experience when you have disconnected? How do you feel?

Ideas for Reflection: A Companion Workbook to *Never Enough - Separating Self-Worth from Approval*
by Deb Lang, PsyD.

chapter five
reflections

Does disconnecting lead you back to appeasing? Think about some examples of this in your life.

Ideas for Reflection: A Companion Workbook to *Never Enough - Separating Self-Worth from Approval* by Deb Lang, PsyD.

chapter five
reflections

Or have you learned to disconnect as a way of avoiding the pull to appease? If so, take a moment to describe when and how you do this.

_____
_____
_____
_____
_____
_____
_____
_____
_____
_____
_____
_____
_____
_____
_____
_____
_____

Ideas for Reflection: A Companion Workbook to *Never Enough - Separating Self-Worth from Approval*
by Deb Lang, PsyD.

chapter six
notes

Ideas for Reflection: A Companion Workbook to *Never Enough - Separating Self-Worth from Approval* by Deb Lang, Psy.D.

chapter six
notes

Ideas for Reflection: A Companion Workbook to *Never Enough - Separating Self-Worth from Approval* by Deb Lang, Psy.D.

chapter six
reflections

Have you been relating to Beth's story? Have you moved far away from your family to be who you want to be in the world? If so, describe what that has been like for you.

chapter six
reflections

Do you find yourself feeling guilty for being far away? When guilt comes up, what do you do?

Ideas for Reflection: A Companion Workbook to *Never Enough - Separating Self-Worth from Approval* by Deb Lang, Psy.D.

chapter six
reflections

When you are around your family of origin, do you hold on to who you are in the world, or do you simply pretend to be who they want you to be until you are back on your own?

Ideas for Reflection: A Companion Workbook to *Never Enough - Separating Self-Worth from Approval* by Deb Lang, Psy.D.

chapter six
reflections

If you are in a relationship, in what ways do the needs of your partner derail you from your efforts to be yourself or to take time for yourself?

Ideas for Reflection: A Companion Workbook to *Never Enough - Separating Self-Worth from Approval*
by Deb Lang, Psy.D.

chapter six
reflections

How might you begin to use the knowledge that these pulls for approval reflect default automatic programming in your brain and not who you are as a person?

chapter seven
notes

Ideas for Reflection: A Companion Workbook to *Never Enough - Separating Self-Worth from Approval*
by Deb Lang, PsyD.

chapter seven
notes

Ideas for Reflection: A Companion Workbook to *Never Enough - Separating Self-Worth from Approval*
by Deb Lang, Psy.D.

chapter seven
reflections

When do you speak up about your needs in a relationship? Do you do so before or after you are at your limit?

Ideas for Reflection: A Companion Workbook to *Never Enough - Separating Self-Worth from Approval* by Deb Lang, Psy.D.

chapter seven
reflections

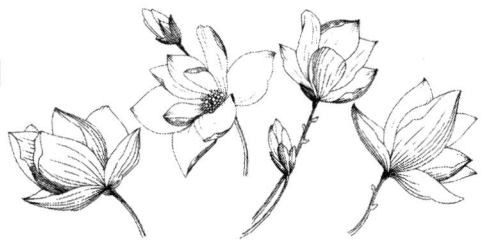

If you speak up or take time for yourself from a place of stress or disconnection, how do you feel afterward?

Ideas for Reflection: A Companion Workbook to *Never Enough - Separating Self-Worth from Approval*
by Deb Lang, Psy.D.

chapter seven
reflections

What examples can you think of in your own life, of a behavior, a thought, or a feeling that have become wired together?

Ideas for Reflection: A Companion Workbook to *Never Enough - Separating Self-Worth from Approval*
by Deb Lang, Psy.D.

chapter eight
notes

Ideas for Reflection: A Companion Workbook to *Never Enough - Separating Self-Worth from Approval*
by Deb Lang, Psy.D.

chapter eight
notes

Ideas for Reflection: A Companion Workbook to *Never Enough - Separating Self-Worth from Approval*
by Deb Lang, Psy.D.

chapter eight
reflections

In what relationships do you feel the pull to appease?

chapter eight
reflections

Does this happen only with people you care about, or do you find yourself trying to keep everyone happy?

Ideas for Reflection: A Companion Workbook to *Never Enough - Separating Self-Worth from Approval*
by Deb Lang, PsyD.

chapter eight
reflections

If you don't work hard to keep people happy what happens for you when you sense that someone is displeased with you?

Ideas for Reflection: A Companion Workbook to *Never Enough - Separating Self-Worth from Approval* by Deb Lang, PsyD.

chapter eight
reflections

Think about whether there are times when you tend to keep yourself at a distance, so you don't feel the pull to appease. If so, in what types of situations or relationships does this happen?

chapter nine
notes

Ideas for Reflection: A Companion Workbook to *Never Enough - Separating Self-Worth from Approval*
by Deb Lang, Psy.D.

chapter nine
notes

Ideas for Reflection: A Companion Workbook to *Never Enough - Separating Self-Worth from Approval*
by Deb Lang, Psy.D.

chapter nine
reflections

Spend some time thinking about the ways the beliefs of an entangled intimacy style have pulled you to look outside of yourself to determine your worth.

Ideas for Reflection: A Companion Workbook to *Never Enough - Separating Self-Worth from Approval* by Deb Lang, Psy.D.

chapter nine
reflections

In what ways does looking outside of yourself for your worth impact your sense of security?

Ideas for Reflection: A Companion Workbook to *Never Enough - Separating Self-Worth from Approval*
by Deb Lang, Psy.D.

chapter nine
reflections

What comes up when you think about separating your self-worth from the reactions of others?

Ideas for Reflection: A Companion Workbook to *Never Enough - Separating Self-Worth from Approval* by Deb Lang, Psy.D.

chapter ten
notes

Ideas for Reflection: A Companion Workbook to *Never Enough - Separating Self-Worth from Approval*
by Deb Lang, Psy.D.

chapter ten
notes

Ideas for Reflection: A Companion Workbook to *Never Enough - Separating Self-Worth from Approval* by Deb Lang, Psy.D.

chapter ten
reflections

What comes up for you when you think about being in the middle in relationships—aware of your feelings and needs as well as those of the other person?

chapter ten
reflections

Take a moment to think of a situation and how you might react to it when you are in the middle with your thinking brain, or "rider," fully engaged and how you might react in that same situation when you are tipped and the "beast" is running the show.

Look at all the aspects of those experiences and how they might differ. For instance, how would your thinking, feelings, and behaviors be different when you are in the middle versus when you are tipped? How would your body feel?

Ideas for Reflection: A Companion Workbook to *Never Enough - Separating Self-Worth from Approval*

by Deb Lang, Psy.D.

chapter ten
reflections

In considering the differences you noticed between the two states, what might be some clues you can use to notice that you have tipped out of the middle?

Ideas for Reflection: A Companion Workbook to *Never Enough - Separating Self-Worth from Approval*
by Deb Lang, PsyD.

chapter eleven
notes

Ideas for Reflection: A Companion Workbook to *Never Enough - Separating Self-Worth from Approval*
by Deb Lang, Psy.D.

chapter eleven
notes

Ideas for Reflection: A Companion Workbook to *Never Enough - Separating Self-Worth from Approval* by Deb Lang, Psy.D.

chapter eleven
reflections

What fears are coming up as you move into part two and begin the work of separating your worth from the approval of others?

Ideas for Reflection: A Companion Workbook to *Never Enough - Separating Self-Worth from Approval* by Deb Lang, Psy.D.

chapter eleven
reflections

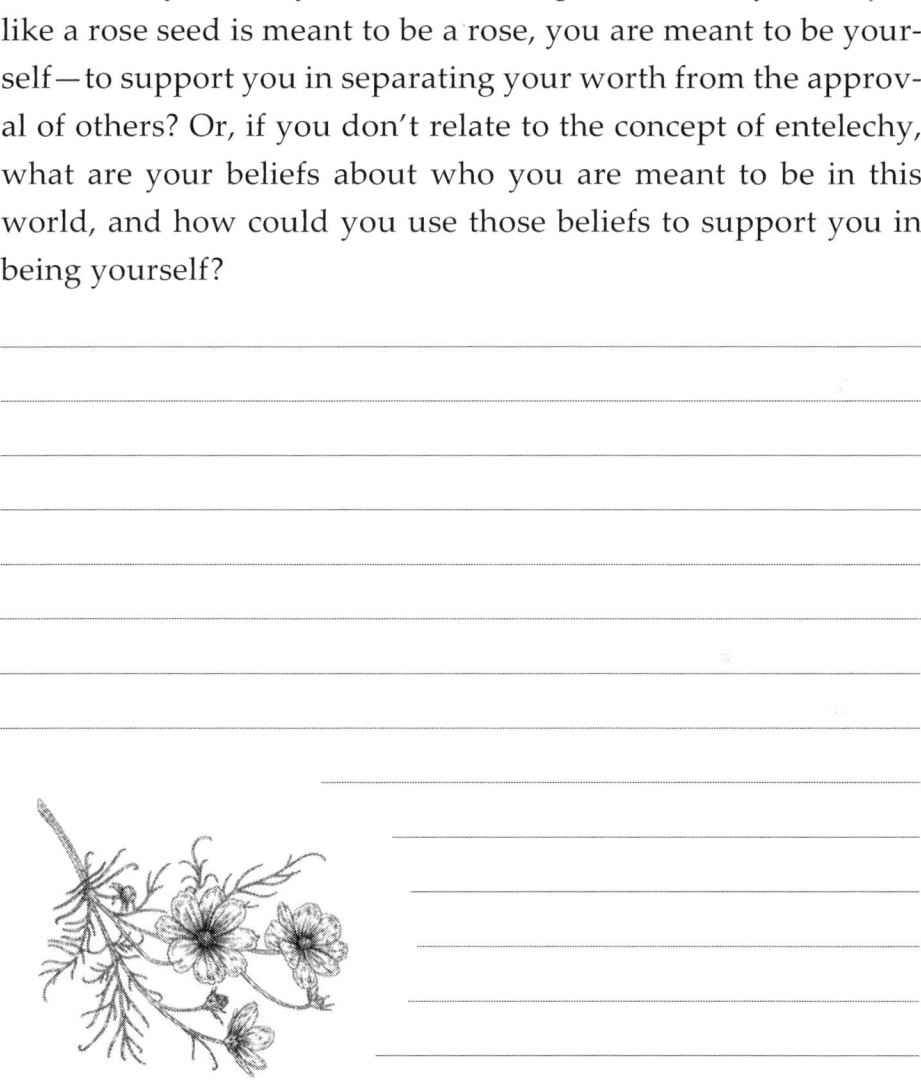

In what ways could you use the concept of entelechy—that just like a rose seed is meant to be a rose, you are meant to be yourself—to support you in separating your worth from the approval of others? Or, if you don't relate to the concept of entelechy, what are your beliefs about who you are meant to be in this world, and how could you use those beliefs to support you in being yourself?

Ideas for Reflection: A Companion Workbook to *Never Enough - Separating Self-Worth from Approval*

by Deb Lang, Psy.D.

chapter eleven
reflections

What did you notice when you connected with your wisest self and/or your entelechy?

Ideas for Reflection: A Companion Workbook to *Never Enough - Separating Self-Worth from Approval*
by Deb Lang, Psy.D.

chapter eleven
reflections

In what ways do you already use your imagination in your life? Think about whether what you imagine calms you or tips you into a stress response.

Ideas for Reflection: A Companion Workbook to *Never Enough - Separating Self-Worth from Approval* by Deb Lang, Psy.D.

chapter twelve
notes

Ideas for Reflection: A Companion Workbook to *Never Enough - Separating Self-Worth from Approval*
by Deb Lang, Psy.D.

chapter twelve
notes

Ideas for Reflection: A Companion Workbook to *Never Enough - Separating Self-Worth from Approval* by Deb Lang, Psy.D.

chapter twelve
reflections

What reactions do you have to bringing your attention back to yourself?

Ideas for Reflection: A Companion Workbook to *Never Enough - Separating Self-Worth from Approval*
by Deb Lang, Psy.D.

chapter twelve
reflections

What feelings came up as you practiced the connecting meditation?

Ideas for Reflection: A Companion Workbook to *Never Enough - Separating Self-Worth from Approval* by Deb Lang, Psy.D.

chapter twelve
reflections

Where in your day will you add connecting with yourself? What will you pair it with? How will you remind yourself to connect?

Ideas for Reflection: A Companion Workbook to *Never Enough - Separating Self-Worth from Approval*
by Deb Lang, Psy.D.

chapter twelve
reflections

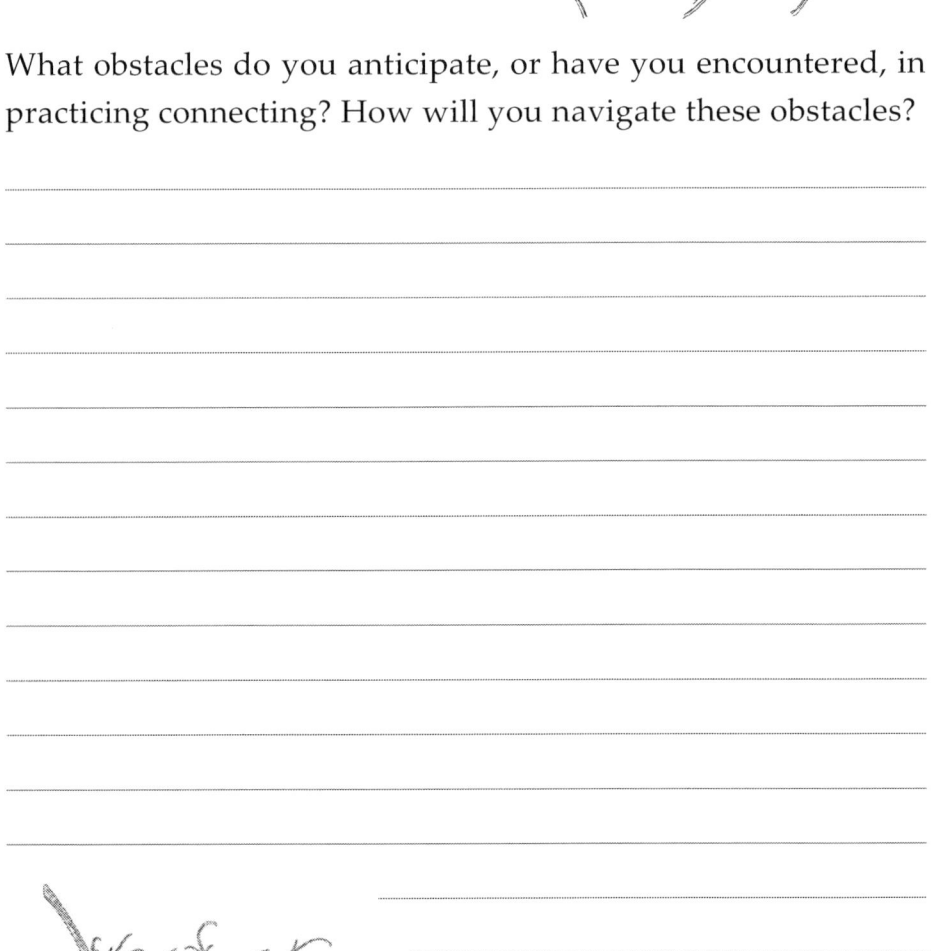

What obstacles do you anticipate, or have you encountered, in practicing connecting? How will you navigate these obstacles?

Ideas for Reflection: A Companion Workbook to *Never Enough - Separating Self-Worth from Approval* by Deb Lang, Psy.D.

chapter twelve
reflections

What did you notice when you used your imagination to mentally rehearse connections with yourself?

Ideas for Reflection: A Companion Workbook to *Never Enough - Separating Self-Worth from Approval*
by Deb Lang, Psy.D.

chapter twelve
reflections

What feelings are coming up as you are paying attention to yourself? Any difficult feelings? How about rewarding feelings?

Ideas for Reflection: A Companion Workbook to *Never Enough - Separating Self-Worth from Approval*
by Deb Lang, Psy.D.

chapter thirteen
notes

Ideas for Reflection: A Companion Workbook to Never Enough - Separating Self-Worth from Approval
by Deb Lang, Psy.D.

chapter thirteen
notes

Ideas for Reflection: A Companion Workbook to *Never Enough - Separating Self-Worth from Approval*
by Deb Lang, Psy.D.

chapter thirteen
reflections

What comes up for you when you think of accepting yourself right now, as you are?

Ideas for Reflection: A Companion Workbook to *Never Enough - Separating Self-Worth from Approval* by Deb Lang, Psy.D.

chapter thirteen
reflections

How about when you think of feeling self-compassion?

Ideas for Reflection: A Companion Workbook to *Never Enough - Separating Self-Worth from Approval* by Deb Lang, Psy.D.

chapter thirteen
reflections

How will you begin adding self-acceptance and compassion to your connections? What do you suppose will make it easier?

Ideas for Reflection: A Companion Workbook to *Never Enough - Separating Self-Worth from Approval*
by Deb Lang, Psy.D.

chapter thirteen
reflections

How might you use imagery to mentally rehearse bringing these skills into your life?

Ideas for Reflection: A Companion Workbook to *Never Enough - Separating Self-Worth from Approval* by Deb Lang, Psy.D.

chapter fourteen
notes

chapter fourteen
notes

chapter fourteen
reflections

What has been your experience with noticing or expressing your feelings? How might your previous experiences impact you as you check in on your feelings?

Ideas for Reflection: A Companion Workbook to *Never Enough - Separating Self-Worth from Approval* by Deb Lang, Psy.D.

chapter fourteen
reflections

What is it like to imagine a part of yourself as being the feeler of your feelings? Did checking in with her help you to identify your feelings? If not, how will you check in on your feelings?

Ideas for Reflection: A Companion Workbook to *Never Enough - Separating Self-Worth from Approval* by Deb Lang, Psy.D.

chapter fourteen
reflections

Were you able to feel compassion for your younger self or the feeler of your feelings? How about a desire to be her advocate?

_____

_____

_____

_____

_____

_____

_____

_____

_____

_____

_____

_____

_____

_____

_____

_____

Ideas for Reflection: A Companion Workbook to *Never Enough - Separating Self-Worth from Approval* by Deb Lang, Psy.D.

chapter fourteen
reflections

What is it like for you to be putting your feelings into words?

Ideas for Reflection: A Companion Workbook to *Never Enough - Separating Self-Worth from Approval*
by Deb Lang, Psy.D.

chapter fourteen
reflections

What patterns, if any, do you notice in checking in with your strongest feeling?

chapter fourteen
reflections

What, if any, unreasonable assumptions did you uncover?

Ideas for Reflection: A Companion Workbook to *Never Enough - Separating Self-Worth from Approval*
by Deb Lang, Psy.D.

chapter fourteen
reflections

Was there a time, during a connection, when you noticed that you were no longer in the middle? What steps did you take when you noticed this?

Ideas for Reflection: A Companion Workbook to *Never Enough - Separating Self-Worth from Approval*
by Deb Lang, PsyD.

chapter fourteen
reflections

When you notice your feelings, are they connected with any sensations in your body?

Ideas for Reflection: A Companion Workbook to *Never Enough - Separating Self-Worth from Approval* by Deb Lang, PsyD.

chapter fourteen
reflections

Is a certain feeling connected with tension in a specific part of your body or a body posture? Noticing this connection will be another way of noticing your feelings in the future. For instance, what is your posture like when you feel sad? Where do you feel it in your body? How about fear and anger?

Ideas for Reflection: A Companion Workbook to *Never Enough - Separating Self-Worth from Approval* by Deb Lang, Psy.D.

chapter fifteen
part one
notes

chapter fifteen
part one
notes

chapter fifteen
part one
reflections

What changes in your self-care might make it easier to stay in the middle or in balance?

Ideas for Reflection: A Companion Workbook to *Never Enough - Separating Self-Worth from Approval*
by Deb Lang, Psy.D.

chapter fifteen
part one
reflections

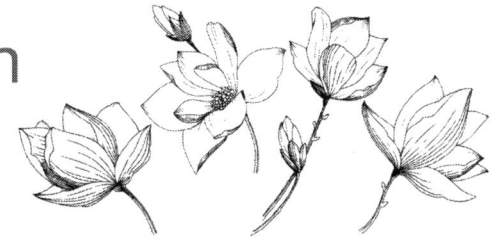

Think of some examples where you kept your finger on the pulse of your inner life and gave yourself what you needed. How about times when you ignored your inner life or checked in with your feelings and didn't follow through? What differences do you notice?

chapter fifteen
part one
reflections

Can you think of an example of a time when a worry came up while you were relaxing? How might the experience be different if you noticed the worry and gave yourself what you needed versus ignoring it?

chapter fifteen
part one
reflections

Pick an example from your life and describe how it would be different when tipped as compared to when you are in balance.

Ideas for Reflection: A Companion Workbook to *Never Enough - Separating Self-Worth from Approval* by Deb Lang, Psy.D.

chapter fifteen
part one
reflections

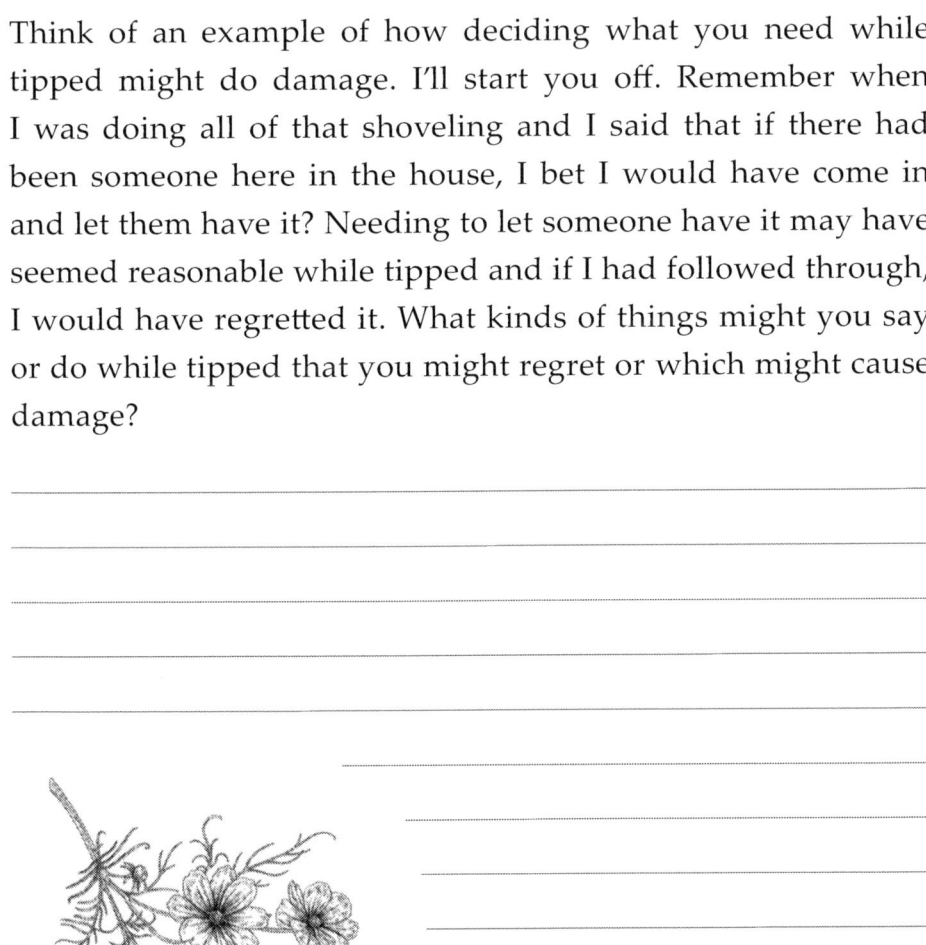

Think of an example of how deciding what you need while tipped might do damage. I'll start you off. Remember when I was doing all of that shoveling and I said that if there had been someone here in the house, I bet I would have come in and let them have it? Needing to let someone have it may have seemed reasonable while tipped and if I had followed through, I would have regretted it. What kinds of things might you say or do while tipped that you might regret or which might cause damage?

_____
_____
_____
_____
_____
_____
_____
_____
_____

Ideas for Reflection: A Companion Workbook to *Never Enough - Separating Self-Worth from Approval* by Deb Lang, Psy.D.

Ideas for Reflection: A Companion Workbook to *Never Enough - Separating Self-Worth from Approval*
by Deb Lang, Psy.D.

chapter fifteen
part one
reflections

Has there been a time when you noticed you were tipped? Please describe and be sure to underline all the work you have done to get to the place where you can notice being tipped! Yahoo!

chapter fifteen
part two
notes

chapter fifteen
part two
notes

chapter fifteen
part two
reflections

What feelings come up when you think about meeting your own needs? Do you feel lost? Is any resentment coming up? If so, describe.

chapter fifteen
part two
reflections

Which feelings are the most difficult for you to figure out what you need? What is it like if you imagine a child in front of you expressing those feelings? Does that make it easier? If you are still stuck, what do you imagine you might say to a friend feeling that feeling?

Ideas for Reflection: A Companion Workbook to *Never Enough - Separating Self-Worth from Approval* by Deb Lang, Psy.D.

chapter fifteen
part two
reflections

If you are checking in on your feelings by imagining a part of you who feels your feelings, do you have a clear image of that part? How old is she? What is she wearing? How long is her hair? Try to really "see" her. If you can't visualize her, no worries. What is your sense of what she is like?

_____
_____
_____
_____
_____
_____
_____
_____
_____
_____
_____
_____
_____

Ideas for Reflection: A Companion Workbook to *Never Enough - Separating Self-Worth from Approval*
by Deb Lang, Psy.D.

chapter fifteen
part two
reflections

After you offered yourself what you needed, how did the feeler of your feelings respond? Did what you offered calm her? If not, what might?

chapter fifteen
part two
reflections

If you are unable to answer the question of what you need, you have most likely slipped out of the middle. What might help you come back into balance? No worries if you are stuck, we will explore how old expectations can keep us fired up in the next section.

chapter fifteen
part three
notes

Ideas for Reflection: A Companion Workbook to *Never Enough - Separating Self-Worth from Approval* by Deb Lang, Psy.D.

chapter fifteen
part three
notes

chapter fifteen
part three
reflections

What old, outdated assumptions have you noticed by identifying your feelings or at times when you were tipped? Write them down so you can watch for them. Identify the kinds of thoughts and feelings that come up when these wires are fired up and write them down as well. Doing so will help you notice when they are "hot" and will give you the opportunity to bring in new information.

_____
_____
_____
_____
_____
_____
_____
_____
_____
_____

Ideas for Reflection: A Companion Workbook to *Never Enough - Separating Self-Worth from Approval* by Deb Lang, Psy.D.

Ideas for Reflection: A Companion Workbook to *Never Enough - Separating Self-Worth from Approval*
by Deb Lang, Psy.D.

chapter fifteen
part three
reflections

What is the new information that needs to come into these wires? What are the facts—not what feels true—the facts? What would you tell your daughter or a good friend?

Ideas for Reflection: A Companion Workbook to *Never Enough - Separating Self-Worth from Approval* by Deb Lang, Psy.D.

chapter fifteen
part three
reflections

In stating that new information, do you believe what you are saying? Can you feel the truth or reward? If not, back up. What do you notice if you accept and feel compassion for where you are right now, even if you still believe the information on the old wire? How does your body feel when you offer yourself that caring?

Ideas for Reflection: A Companion Workbook to *Never Enough - Separating Self-Worth from Approval* by Deb Lang, Psy.D.

chapter fifteen
part four
notes

Ideas for Reflection: A Companion Workbook to Never Enough - Separating Self-Worth from Approval
by Deb Lang, Psy.D.

chapter fifteen
part four
notes

Ideas for Reflection: A Companion Workbook to *Never Enough - Separating Self-Worth from Approval* by Deb Lang, Psy.D.

chapter fifteen
part four
reflections

How has it been to give yourself what you need? What feelings have come up around doing this?

chapter fifteen
part four
reflections

What reactions come up in thinking about communicating a request?

chapter fifteen
part four
reflections

When you think about saying "no," do you notice any core assumptions about yourself or about what would happen if you disagreed?

chapter fifteen
part four
reflections

What is a small step you could take to begin communicating what you need or in saying "no" when a request is not in your best interest?

chapter fifteen
part four
reflections

Take time to feel love and compassion for yourself. Wherever you are in this process, it is right for you in the present moment and means nothing about what is possible in the future.

Ideas for Reflection: A Companion Workbook to *Never Enough - Separating Self-Worth from Approval* by Deb Lang, Psy.D.

chapter sixteen
notes

Ideas for Reflection: A Companion Workbook to *Never Enough - Separating Self-Worth from Approval*
by Deb Lang, Psy.D.

chapter sixteen
notes

Ideas for Reflection: A Companion Workbook to Never Enough - Separating Self-Worth from Approval
by Deb Lang, PsyD.

chapter sixteen
reflections

What brings you joy?

_____

_____

_____

_____

_____

_____

_____

_____

_____

_____

_____

_____

_____

_____

_____

_____

_____

Ideas for Reflection: A Companion Workbook to *Never Enough - Separating Self-Worth from Approval*
by Deb Lang, Psy.D.

chapter sixteen
reflections

What is your passion? Your greater purpose? Your North Star?

Ideas for Reflection: A Companion Workbook to *Never Enough - Separating Self-Worth from Approval*
by Deb Lang, Psy.D.

chapter sixteen
reflections

Take some time to reflect and either write about or illustrate your larger purpose or your destiny—really "paint that picture" with your words or with what you draw.

Ideas for Reflection: A Companion Workbook to *Never Enough - Separating Self-Worth from Approval*
by Deb Lang, Psy.D.

chapter sixteen
reflections

What do you notice when you think about and or paint the picture of your larger purpose? Do any painful feelings come up, like fear or guilt? If so, look for an unreasonable assumption beneath these feelings.

chapter sixteen
reflections

Mentally rehearse the experience of your destiny or larger purpose. Be in the experience, making sure to feel the reward feelings that you will be feeling as you align with your greater purpose.

Ideas for Reflection: A Companion Workbook to *Never Enough - Separating Self-Worth from Approval* by Deb Lang, Psy.D.

chapter sixteen
reflections

What is a first step you will take, no matter how small, to move you closer to your destiny?

Ideas for Reflection: A Companion Workbook to *Never Enough - Separating Self-Worth from Approval* by Deb Lang, Psy.D.

chapter seventeen
notes

Ideas for Reflection: A Companion Workbook to *Never Enough - Separating Self-Worth from Approval* by Deb Lang, Psy.D.

chapter seventeen
notes

Ideas for Reflection: A Companion Workbook to *Never Enough - Separating Self-Worth from Approval* by Deb Lang, PsyD.

chapter seventeen
reflections

What bumps do you expect to encounter as you work on separating your worth from the approval of others?

chapter seventeen
reflections

How will you encourage yourself to keep practicing?

Ideas for Reflection: A Companion Workbook to *Never Enough - Separating Self-Worth from Approval*
by Deb Lang, Psy.D.

chapter seventeen
reflections

What support might you need?

Ideas for Reflection: A Companion Workbook to *Never Enough - Separating Self-Worth from Approval*
by Deb Lang, Psy.D.

chapter eighteen
notes

Ideas for Reflection: A Companion Workbook to *Never Enough - Separating Self-Worth from Approval*
by Deb Lang, Psy.D.

chapter eighteen
notes

Ideas for Reflection: A Companion Workbook to *Never Enough - Separating Self-Worth from Approval*
by Deb Lang, Psy.D.

chapter eighteen
reflections

What feelings came up for you as you read these women's stories?

Ideas for Reflection: A Companion Workbook to *Never Enough - Separating Self-Worth from Approval*
by Deb Lang, Psy.D.

chapter eighteen
reflections

Did you notice any old wires of comparison coming up?

chapter eighteen
reflections

If so, take a moment to feel compassion for yourself. It is natural that these wires would light up. This is a moment of opportunity to bring some new information into these wires. See if you can identify the core unreasonable assumptions. What new information needs to come into these wires?

Ideas for Reflection: A Companion Workbook to *Never Enough - Separating Self-Worth from Approval*
by Deb Lang, PsyD.

chapter nineteen
notes

Ideas for Reflection: A Companion Workbook to *Never Enough - Separating Self-Worth from Approval*
by Deb Lang, Psy.D.

chapter nineteen
notes

Ideas for Reflection: A Companion Workbook to *Never Enough - Separating Self-Worth from Approval*
by Deb Lang, Psy.D.

chapter nineteen
reflections

What thoughts and emotions are coming up as you finish this book?

Ideas for Reflection: A Companion Workbook to *Never Enough - Separating Self-Worth from Approval*
by Deb Lang, Psy.D.

chapter nineteen
reflections

What are you feeling inspired to do?

Ideas for Reflection: A Companion Workbook to *Never Enough - Separating Self-Worth from Approval* by Deb Lang, Psy.D.

chapter nineteen
reflections

What small change might you make that might over time grow into a well-traveled highway?

Ideas for Reflection: A Companion Workbook to *Never Enough - Separating Self-Worth from Approval*
by Deb Lang, Psy.D.

chapter nineteen
reflections

How might your work on being yourself in the world inspire or support other women in being themselves in the world?

Ideas for Reflection: A Companion Workbook to *Never Enough - Separating Self-Worth from Approval*
by Deb Lang, PsyD.

Made in United States
Orlando, FL
22 March 2025